W9-BRH-215

# STARTING HISTORY

# The Greeks

Written by Sally Hewitt

A+

**Smart Apple Media**

This book has been published in cooperation with Franklin Watts.

**Editor:** Rachel Tonkin, **Designers:** Rachel Hamdi and
Holly Fulbrook, **Picture researcher:** Diana Morris,
**Craft models made by:** Anna-Marie D'Cruz

**Picture credits**
Martin Bond/SPL: 24b; British Museum, London/HIP/Topfoto: 8bl,
10cl, 11t, 13t, 14b; Dagli Orti/Art Archive: 10tr; HIP/Topfoto: 9t,
17b, 22t; Kanellopoulos Museum, Athens/Dagli Orti/Art Archive:
7b; Hervé Lewandowski/Photo RMN: front cover t; Musée du
Louvre, Paris/Dagli Orti/Art Archive: 8tr, 21t; Musée du Louvre,
Paris/Erich Lessing/AKG Images: 12, 14t; Museo Capitalino,
Rome/Dagli Orti/Art Archive: 20b; Museo Nazionale Romano,
Rome/Dagli Orti/Art Archive: 26b; National Archaeological
Museum, Athens/Dagli Orti/Art Archive: 7t; Picturepoint/Topfoto:
15t, 25t; Jose Fuste Raga/Corbis: 22b; Pete Saloutos/Corbis: 18;
Topfoto: 16tr, 24t; Roger-Viollet/Topfoto: 16bl, 17t; Chris
Fairclough: 27.

All other images: Steve Shott

With thanks to our models Maria Cheung and Ryan Lovett

Published in the United States by Smart Apple Media
2140 Howard Drive West, North Mankato, Minnesota 56003

U.S. publication copyright © 2008 Smart Apple Media
International copyright reserved in all countries. No part of this
book may be reproduced in any form without written permission
from the publisher.
Printed in the United States

Library of Congress Cataloging-in-Publication Data

Hewitt, Sally, 1949–
The Greeks / by Sally Hewitt.
p. cm. — (Starting history)
Includes index.
ISBN-13: 978-1-59920-045-3
1. Greece—Civilization—To 146 B.C.—Juvenile literature. I. Title.

DF77.H58 2007
938—dc22        2006034722

9 8 7 6 5 4 3 2 1

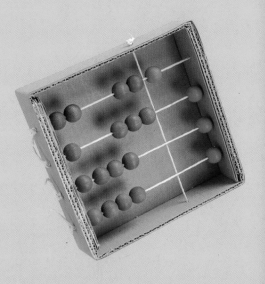

# Contents

# The Greeks

The ancient Greeks lived on mainland Greece and its many surrounding islands in the Mediterranean Sea.

## Ancient Greece

Ancient Greeks began to build cities as early as 1700 B.C. Their civilization lasted for more than 2,000 years. In 146 B.C., Greece became part of the **Roman Empire**. The Romans took on many Greek ideas.

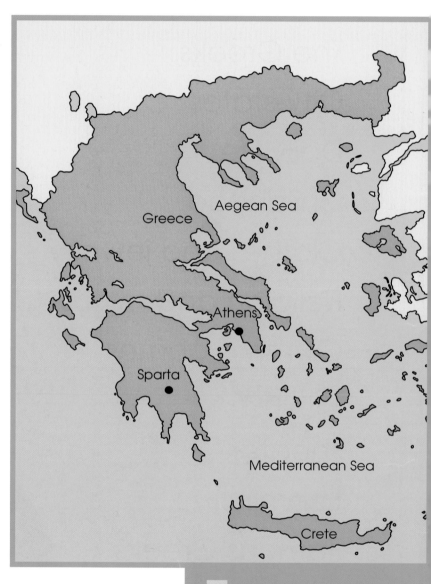

Greece

Aegean Sea

Athens

Sparta

Mediterranean Sea

Crete

Cities grew up around ports and wherever there was good farming land.

## Climate

The **climate** of ancient Greece was hot and dry. Mountains made it difficult to travel on land. People lived along the coast and traveled by sea.

## Trade and travel

The Greeks were sailors. They became rich and successful through trade with other Mediterranean countries. Grain was imported from the Black Sea, timber from Italy, and gems, **ivory**, **linen**, and **papyrus** from Egypt.

The Greeks were famous for their architecture. This is an ancient Greek model for a building.

## Democracy

The ancient Greeks had a rich **culture** of learning, art, and **architecture**. They had a system of **government** called a **democracy**, which means "rule by the people."

Today, countries all over the world have governments based on ancient Greek democracy.

The ancient Greeks wore loose clothes, leather sandals, and hats to protect themselves from the hot sun.

# City-states

Ancient Greece was broken up into a series of city-states. A city-state was made up of the city and its surrounding countryside.

## Athens

The city-state of Athens was a center of culture and learning. It was near the sea and surrounded by **fertile** valleys. Silver, lead, and marble from the nearby hills made Athens rich. A strong **navy** helped to make it powerful.

## Sparta

The city-state of Sparta was warlike. All young men were trained as soldiers, and the Spartan army was known for its toughness and bravery. Much of the work in both Sparta and Athens was done by slaves.

## War

Athens and Sparta were rivals. They fought against each other in the Peloponnesian War, which lasted for 27 years, from 431 to 404 B.C. The war divided ancient Greece and made it weak.

This image of a slave girl serving her master appears on an ancient Greek cup.

## Parthenon

The Parthenon was built in 438 B.C. to celebrate the glory of Athens. Classical Greek architecture such as this has been copied all over the world.

The ruins of the Parthenon can be seen on a hill above Athens.

# Make a model of the Parthenon

▶ 1 Draw the front view of the Parthenon on white cardboard, adding tabs at the top. Allow an extra panel along the bottom to fold back. Carefully cut it out.

▶ 2 Using a light-colored, felt-tipped pen, draw the grooves on the pillars and the decorations on the roof.

▶ 3 Fold a strip of cardboard

like a fan for the steps. Glue it onto the front of the Parthenon.

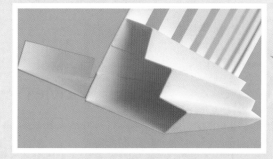

▶ 4 Fold back the tabs and glue them onto blue cardboard to give a 3-D effect.

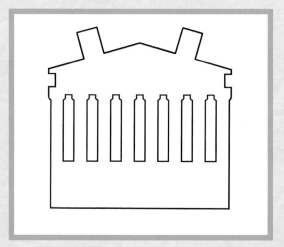

# Daily life

Greek houses were made of mud bricks and plaster, with clay tiles on the roofs. Rooms were arranged around a courtyard with a well in the center. Windows were small with wooden shutters to keep out the hot sun.

This is an early ancient Greek house, preserved by a volcano eruption on the Greek island of Santorini.

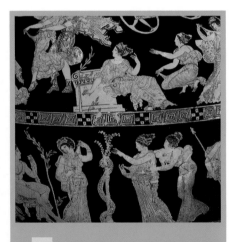
This vase shows what Greek women looked like.

## Men and women

Men were **citizens** with the right to vote and work. Women could not vote and had to obey their husbands. They looked after the home and spent their time caring for their children, cooking, **spinning**, and weaving.

## Food

People ate porridge, bread, figs, grapes, and olives, which all grew locally. Goats provided milk and cheese, and hens provided eggs. In poorer homes, meat was only eaten on feast days, but there was plenty of fish. Wealthier Greeks hunted deer and **boar**.

## Pottery

Pots were made to store food and drink. They had many different shapes.

An amphora was a storage jar with two handles used for wine, oil, and olives; a hydria was a jug with three handles used for carrying and pouring water; and a kylix was a drinking cup.

Black figure pots had black figures painted onto the red clay. On red figure pots, the background was painted black.

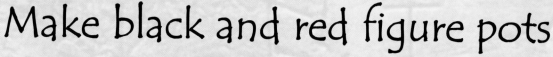

# Make black and red figure pots

▶ 1 Copy this shape onto construction paper. Draw two copies onto orange construction paper and one onto black paper. Make each one as big as this page. Cut out.

▶ 2 Draw a simple shape onto the middle of the black vase shape.

▶ 3 Cut out the simple shape carefully as if it were a stencil. Make one cut from the base to make it easier to cut out.

▶ 4 Glue the cut-out shape onto one orange pot and the outline onto the other orange pot to make one black and one red figure pot.

# Childhood

In ancient Greece, boys and girls were brought up differently. Girls stayed at home, where their mothers taught them how to run the house. Only a few had lessons. Boys went to school. Only sons could inherit the family wealth. They grew up to be citizens and soldiers.

## Toys and games

Greek children played with wooden carts, spinning tops, hoops, yo-yos, and dolls. They played games called tag and blind-man's bluff and a game similar to baseball.

## Growing up

When children were 12 or 13, boys gave up their toys to the god Apollo and girls to the goddess Artemis to show that their childhood was over.

Ancient Greek clay doll with moveable legs.

Children played with the knucklebones of small animals. The games were similar to the ones played with modern jacks.

Both adults and children enjoyed playing knucklebones.

# Make and play knucklebones

▶ 1 Tear up newspaper and put the pieces into a bowl of water and craft glue.

▶ 2 Squeeze the water out to make small lumps of papier mâché.

Curl your fingers around each lump to make a knucklebone shape.

▶ 3 Let the knucklebones dry thoroughly.

▶ 4 Paint yellow and varnish with a layer of watered-down craft glue.

## How to play knucklebones

### Game A (6 bones)

Spread the fingers of one hand on the ground. Throw one bone in the air with the other hand. Try to knock another bone into a space between your fingers before you catch it. Try to get all five bones in place.

### Game B

Throw the bones in the air and catch as many as you can on the back of your hand.

# Clothes and jewelry

This picture on a Greek vase shows a woman holding up her mirror and her jewelry box.

Ancient Greek clothes were light and comfortable. They were made of fine wool or linen. The rich wore **silk** from China.

## Daily wear

Men and women wore a chiton, which was a **tunic** fastened with brooches at the shoulders and a belt around the waist. A cloak called a himation was worn around the shoulders. Children wore short tunics.

## Hair and makeup

Women took pride in their looks. They had elaborate hair styles. Mirrors and pots have been found that tell us they wore makeup and perfume. Both men and women wore sun hats.

An ancient Greek perfume bottle made to look like a lion.

Ancient Greek earrings. The ones on the left have cockle shells hanging from them.

## Jewelry

Jewelry was a sign of wealth and status. The rich wore gold and silver. The less wealthy had jewelry made of bronze, lead, iron, and glass. People were buried with their most

# Make gold earrings

▶ **1** Cut eight two-inch (5 cm) lengths and two four-inch (10 cm) lengths of gold string.

▶ **2** Copy the shapes below onto thin, gold cardboard and cut them out. Score on patterns with a blunt pencil and cut out.

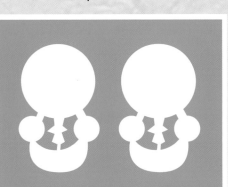

▶ **3** Make a hole at the top of the large circle shapes and four holes along the bottom of each earring.

▶ **4** Thread short gold string through each of the holes along the bottom and tie. Attach a bead and knot.

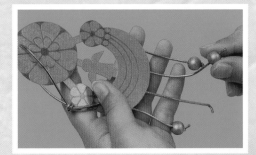

▶ **5** Thread gold string through the top holes of both earrings to make loops. Hang them over your ears.

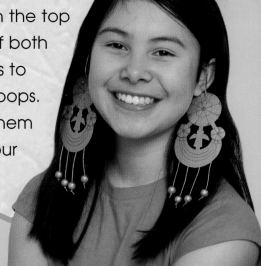

# Religion and myths

The Greeks worshipped many gods and goddesses. Public festivals were held to make the gods happy so they would grant the people's wishes and protect them from danger. A festival could be a play, an athletic competition, or a procession.

This temple in Agrigento is almost exactly as it was when it was first built by the ancient Greeks.

A statue of the king of the gods, Zeus.

## Temples

Temples were the most magnificent buildings in the city. A temple was a god's home on Earth. People brought animals or birds to the temple, where a priest **sacrificed** them to the gods.

Each home had its own small **altar** where the family worshipped every day.

## Myths

**Myths** are stories about gods, goddesses, and heroes that teach important lessons about life.

16

## Myth of Icarus

Icarus's father Daedalus made his son wings of wax and feathers. He warned Icarus not to fly too close to the sun. But Icarus disobeyed, the wax melted, and he fell to his death. What do you think the lesson of this myth was?

# Make a collage of Icarus

Draw Icarus with his wings. Draw the sun in the background. Glue pieces of material on Icarus and feathers on Icarus's wings. Cut out yellow construction paper in the shape of a sun. Glue it over the sun you drew to finish the picture.

# Olympic games

The Greeks believed that the gods lived on Mount Olympus and that Zeus was their ruler. Games were held at Olympia every four years in honor of Zeus. The games were so important that all wars were stopped while they took place.

Discus-throwing was one of the events at the ancient Greek Olympic Games.

## Olympia
At Olympia, there was a building for each event.

## Marathon
In 490 B.C., the Greeks defeated Persian invaders at the battle of Marathon. A messenger ran 26 miles (41 km) from Marathon to Athens to deliver the good news. He then collapsed and died. The marathon became part of the modern Olympic Games when they were started in 1896.

Palaistra—wrestling and jumping

Gymnasium—training and throwing

Stadium—track events

Races were held in a stadium, such as this one at Delphi.

Relay races were held at night. Runners passed torches instead of batons. The winner lit a fire on an altar to the gods.

◻ An athlete uses the torch to light the Olympic flame to start the modern Olympic Games.

# Make an Olympic torch

▶ **1** Draw the shapes below onto construction paper: draw shape A onto silver paper and shape B onto gold paper. Roll

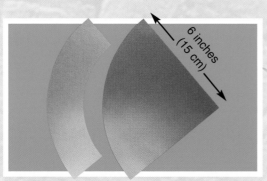

6 inches (15 cm)

shape B into a cone and glue. Glue the silver paper around the top of the cone.

▶ **2** Cut flames of red, yellow, and orange tissue paper; use white and gray for smoke. Glue them inside your torch.

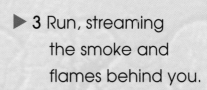

▶ **3** Run, streaming the smoke and flames behind you.

# Writing

The word "alphabet" comes from the first two letters of the Greek alphabet—alpha and beta. The Greeks were the first to write vowels—A, E, I, O, and U.

## The Greek alphabet

| | | | | | | | | | |
|---|---|---|---|---|---|---|---|---|---|
| α | **A** | Alpha a | ι | **I** | Iota i | ρ | **P** | Rho r |
| β | **B** | Beta b | κ | **K** | Kappa k | σ ς | **Σ** | Sigma s |
| γ | **Γ** | Gamma g | λ | **Λ** | Lambda l | τ | **T** | Tau t |
| δ | **Δ** | Delta d | μ | **M** | Muf m | υ | **Υ** | Upsilon u/y |
| ε | **E** | Epsilon e | ν | **N** | Nu n | φ | **Φ** | Phi f |
| ζ | **Z** | Zeta z | ξ | **Ξ** | Xi x | χ | **X** | Chi ch |
| η | **H** | Eta e | ο | **O** | Omicron o | ψ | **Ψ** | Psi ps |
| θ | **Θ** | Theta th | π | **Π** | Pi p | ω | **Ω** | Omega o |

## Homer

The Greek poet Homer is famous for his poems the *Iliad*—the story of the siege of Troy—and the *Odyssey*—the story of Odysseus's journey home from Troy to the island of Ithaca. Homer knew the poems by heart and never wrote them down. The copies we have of his poems were written down hundreds of years after his death.

A statue of Homer, the famous poet.

20

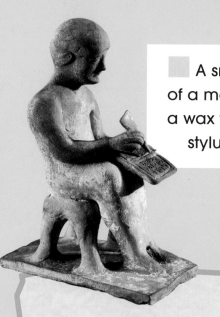

A small figure of a man writing on a wax tablet with a stylus.

## Wax tablets and scrolls

Boys learned to write at school. They scratched letters onto a wax tablet with a pointed stylus. Poems were written on scrolls of papyrus, which was a kind off paper made from reeds.

# Write in Greek letters

Write the name Odysseus in Greek letters and draw a picture of one of his adventures.

Now write your own name. Look for the story of Odysseus in books or on the Internet. Try *Greek Myths* by Geraldine McCaughrean.

Οδυσσευσ

# Theater

Theaters were built all over the Greek world, and many are still there today. A theater could hold thousands of people. Everyone could see the stage and hear the actors and musicians clearly.

A carving of a mask used in an ancient Greek comedy.

## Plays

Plays were performed in honor of the gods. When a religious festival was held, everyone had days off so they could see the plays. Tragedies were plays about heroes and gods. Comedies were about everyday life.

## Actors

The actors were all men. They wore masks so that they could be seen from the back of the theater. The masks had open mouths that made the actor's voice louder.

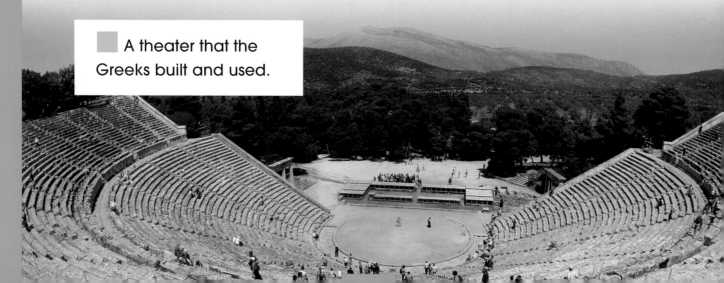

A theater that the Greeks built and used.

# Make Greek theater masks

▶ **1** Copy the outlines of the masks below onto construction paper. Make them as big as your face. Cut them out, leaving a tab at each side.

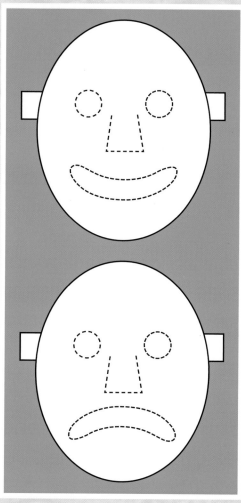

▶ **4** Paint the mask, adding white around the eyes.

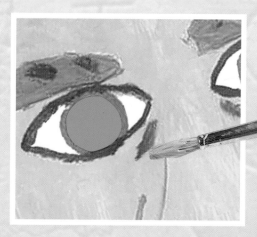

▶ **5** All kinds of materials can be added for hair—wool, cotton balls, shaggy material, or strips of tissue paper.

▶ **6** Tie string through the holes in the tabs and wear.

▶ **2** Cut out the eyes, mouth, and nose flap. Punch a hole in the tabs at the sides.

▶ **3** Build up eyebrows and a nose with papier mâché.

# Learning

Traditionally, the Greeks learned about life, death, and the world around themselves from their gods, myths, and legends. Eventually, however, they began to look for practical knowledge through studying history and carrying out experiments.

A bust of Pythagoras, a mathematician who devised a theory that is still used in geometry.

## Philosophers

Socrates, Aristotle, and Plato were philosophers, meaning "lovers of knowledge." They explored the way people lived and how states were run.

A water treatment plant that uses Archimedes's invention.

## Historians

History was written down by historians, such as Herodotus and Xenophon, so that lessons could be learned from real events.

## Scientists

The scientist Archimedes invented a screw pump that lifts water from a river for irrigating fields. Screw pumps are still used today.

Numbers were calculated using a simple abacus made from lines in the sand and counters.

Modern abacuses are made with wood and beads.

# Make an abacus from a small box and beads

▶ 1 Use the lid from a small cardboard box. Make four holes in each side, about one inch (2.5 cm) apart.

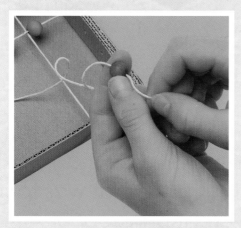

▶ 2 Thread string through the holes, lacing four blue beads and one red bead on each as you go, and tie in place.

▶ 3 Make a hole in the top and bottom of the box, as shown, and thread a piece of string from top to bottom.

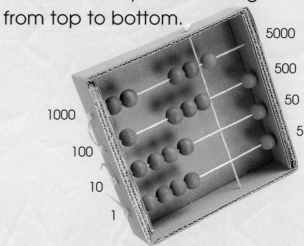

The blue beads are worth 1, 10, 100, and 1,000 from bottom to top, and the red beads are worth 5, 50, 500, and 5,000.

The beads pushed to the middle show the number being made.

Can you see how this is 7,300?

25

# Famous Greeks

Many famous ancient Greeks live on in their **achievements**, their inventions, or their ideas.

### Alexander the Great (356–323 B.C.)

Alexander the Great was a brilliant general who died when he was only 32. He conquered lands from Greece to India and made the biggest empire in the ancient world.

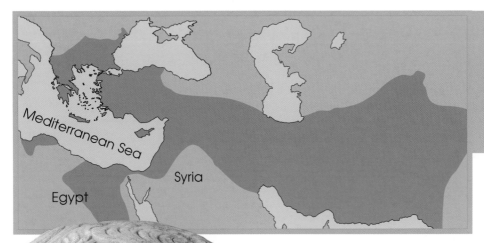

The areas in dark purple show the lands that Alexander conquered.

### Aristotle (384–322 B.C.)

Alexander the Great was taught by the great philosopher Aristotle. Aristotle is known for having studied almost every subject possible at the time. He wrote many books on different subjects.

A bust of Aristotle. Aristotle was taught by another famous Greek philosoper, Plato.

# Hippocrates (460–380 B.C.)

Hippocrates was a doctor. He based his work on practical study of his patients. He discovered that willow bark contained the pain killer we know as aspirin.

Hippocrates believed that all doctors should put the care and good health of their patients first. Until recently, doctors used to take the Hippocratic oath to promise that they would do this.

Modern doctors do not take the Hippocratic oath anymore, but they still make a similar promise that they will look after their patients.

# Sappho (c. 630–570 B.C.)

Sappho was a poetess who wrote about family and friends instead of heroic tales of men and gods. She ran a school for girls and was one of the great poets of her time.

# Glossary

**Achievement**

Something that somebody has worked hard at and done successfully.

**Altar**

A table on which sacrifices to the gods were made.

**Architecture**

The design and construction of buildings.

**Boar**

A wild pig hunted by the Greeks for food.

**Citizen**

A free man who could vote and take part in the government of his city-state.

**Climate**

The kind of weather that an area has.

**Culture**

The art, music, thinking, and learning of a nation or group of people.

**Democracy**

A system of government that is voted for and run by the people.

**Fertile**

A word that describes soil in which crops grow well.

**Government**

A group of people who make laws and run a country.

**Ivory**

Material that comes from elephant tusks and is carved to make jewelry, combs, and mirrors.

## Linen

Cloth woven from threads spun from the flax plant.

## Myth

A traditional story about gods and heroes.

## Navy

A group of ships and the people trained to use them for fighting.

## Papyrus

Paper made from the papyrus reed.

## Roman Empire

A group of countries ruled by the Roman emperor.

## Sacrifice

An offering to the gods. Gifts of food or animals were brought to the temple to be killed to please the gods.

## Silk

A fine cloth spun from threads made by silkworms.

## Spinning

Twisting wool or linen into long, thin threads.

## Tunic

A loose piece of knee-length clothing worn with a belt around the waist.

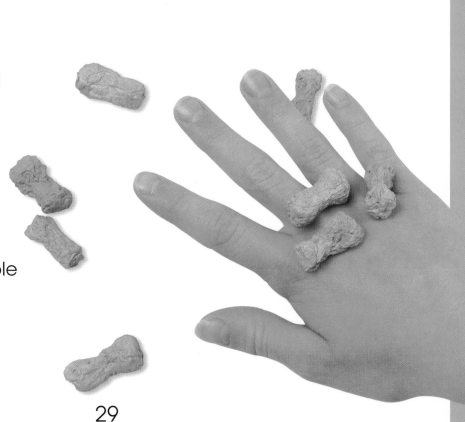

# Index